GW01552887

# The Cancer Woman

The Ca

Ariel Books

**Andrews McMeel
Publishing**

Kansas City

# ncer
## Woman

### June 22–July 23

Julie Mars

Illustrated by Sarah Hollander

ISBN: 0-7407-1429-5
Library of Congress Catalog Card Number: 00-106904

designed by Junie Lee
typeset by Ellen M. Carnahan

# Contents

# Introduction

Did you ever wish upon a star? Have you ever studied the night sky, transfixed by its vast beauty and magnificent mystery?

Astrologers believe that the celestial bodies overhead correspond in some significant way with our own bodies (and personalities) here on Earth.

For more than five thousand years, women have gazed heavenward, searching for connections between the cosmos and their own human minds and spirits. Looking to the planets and stars for guid-

ance in the areas of romance and friendship gives all women a powerful way to
understand and better direct their own
lives and personal destinies.

## PLANETARY RULERS

Astrology is the product of centuries of
precise observation of both the planets
and human nature, yet it also incorpo-
rates a degree of intuition. So when an
astrologer identifies a sun sign, it is much
more than a convenient label. It is a
strong indicator of the particular cosmic

energy that helps shape each woman's personality. There even tends to be a natural affinity between two people born under the same planetary ruler.

*Aries* (March 21–April 20) is ruled by Mars, the planet of forcefulness, physical energy, and sex drive.

*Taurus* (April 21–May 21), like Libra, is ruled by Venus, the planet of love, affection, and pleasure.

*Gemini* (May 22–June 21), like Virgo, is ruled by Mercury, the planet of communication and travel.

*Cancer* (June 22–July 23) is ruled by the Moon, the planet of reflection, cyclical change, and receptivity.

*Leo* (July 24–August 23) is ruled by the Sun, the planet of self-centeredness, brilliance, and warmth.

*Virgo* (August 24–September 23), like Gemini, is ruled by Mercury, the planet of communication and travel.

*Libra* (September 24–October 23), like Taurus, is ruled by Venus, the planet of love, affection, and pleasure.

*Scorpio* (October 24–November 22) is ruled by Pluto, the planet of transformation through the powers of both creativity and destruction.

*Sagittarius* (November 23–December 21) is ruled by Jupiter, the planet of good luck, generosity, and success.

*Capricorn* (December 22–January 20) is ruled by Saturn, the planet of hard work, responsibility, and endurance.

*Aquarius* (January 21–February 19) is ruled by Uranus, the planet of originality, change, and sudden inspiration.

*Pisces* (February 20–March 20) is ruled by Neptune, the planet of illusion, mystery, and the force of imagination.

## ELEMENTS AND QUALITIES

Two other basic concepts are essential to astrological interpretation. The first is called the *element,* of which there are four: *earth, air, fire,* and *water.* Each element carries with it a vast body of associations that help you to understand how your sign interacts with other signs.

*Earth.* This element is often connected with such traits as steadiness, practicality, and predictability. "Earthy" women tend to be firmly rooted and notoriously stable. The three earth signs are Taurus, Virgo, and Capricorn.

*Air.* The signs associated with this element are more likely to be intellectual and analytical. "Airy" women tend to display great emotional detachment and are often described as elusive or unavailable. Gemini, Libra, and Aquarius are the three air signs.

*Fire.* This element is associated with activity, energy, and impulsiveness. "Fiery" women tend to be vivacious, dynamic, optimistic, and domineering. Aries, Leo, and Sagittarius comprise the three fire signs.

*Water.* This element is often associated with emotion and intuition. The water signs are Cancer, Scorpio, and Pisces. "Watery" women tend to be moody, sensitive, creative, and deep.

The final astrological variable is the *quality* of a particular sign. The quality reflects a sun sign's relationship to the rest of the world. There are three qualities: *cardinal,* which initiates change; *mutable,* which adapts to circumstances; and *fixed,* which maintains the status quo. Aries, Cancer, Libra, and Capricorn are outgoing, energetic cardinal signs. Taurus, Leo, Scorpio, and Aquarius are fixed, or resistant. Gemini, Virgo, Sagittarius, and Pisces are flexible, or mutable.

Each sign is a unique combination of quality and element. Because of this specificity, women can glean much personal information from even a minor astrological analysis. The complex art of astrology, with its mix of science and subjectivity, offers all women insight into the present … and a hint or two about the future!

# Just the Facts on Cancer

| | |
|---|---|
| Motto: | "I feel" |
| Element: | Water |
| Quality: | Cardinal |
| Opposite Sign: | Capricorn |
| Ruling Planet: | The Moon |
| Animals: | All creatures with shells |
| Jewel: | Pearl |
| Numbers: | Three and seven |

# Your Sun Sign Profile

## CANCER

The Moon, which symbolizes cyclical change and receptivity, rules the sign of Cancer. And Cancerian women typically embody these heavenly attributes—in the form of whimsy, moodiness, and an often infallible intuitive streak.

Perhaps the key words "I feel" provide a clue to the ever-changing, yet serenely stable Cancer personality. The Crab is forever rocked by inner waves of powerful emotions that rise and fall like the tides under the Moon's mysterious attraction. Because she is watery by nature, she may be given to strange fits of teariness. Her heart is tender, and she seems to absorb both the pain and joy around her.

Because of her extreme sensitivity, the Cancerian woman sometimes protects herself by developing a hard outer shell. This veneer of toughness (and her occasional cranky moods) can fool the casual observer into thinking she is standoffish. It's simply not true! The typical Cancerian

woman is just the opposite—shy, gentle, sweet, and fragile.

Like the crab that symbolizes her sun sign, the Cancerian woman likes to hold on—tight. She deeply values connection and closeness, and *forever* is often her favorite word. Like the Moon, she is timeless—and proves it by collecting (and keeping) mementos and souvenirs even from childhood. Each sentimental attachment is a beautiful ribbon that happily secures for her both the intimacy of the moment and the memory of the past.

The typical Cancerian woman defines

herself as a daydreamer *and* a pragmatist: Security, with a dash of poetry, is the combination that makes her truly happy. When either is lacking, she must fight a tendency to brood or even sulk. Family, friends, and lovers should learn to sit tight during her dark moods. They will pass!

Unpredictable, imaginative, and insightful, the Cancerian woman is a mystery that others will try to solve. And that's what her magnetism is all about!

# Cancer and Friends

### Cancer Woman/Aries Friends

There is a strong affinity here, but the Ram must learn to curb its sharp tongue and the Crab must try not to retreat too often into its protective shell.

### Cancer Woman/Taurus Friends

Both are security minded and domestic, which leads to natural camaraderie. The Bull's occasional temper tantrums, however, will likely displease the often insecure Crab.

### Cancer Woman/Gemini Friends

Oversensitive, moody Cancer is likely to find the free-spirited Gemini too thoughtless and fickle. Frustration will soon emerge. Keep the friendship casual.

### Cancer Woman/Cancer Friends

A close bond between two Crabs is likely, but expect plenty of evasive darting and withdrawing into shells. Frequent hurt feelings result from a double dose of sensitivity.

### Cancer Woman/Leo Friends

Leo loves to be the star of the show, and Cancer is usually a perfectly appreciative audience. The chemistry is right for a supereasy friendship.

### Cancer Woman/Virgo Friends

Virgo's sharp words may sometimes threaten (or wound) the vulnerable Crab, but harmony can be quickly restored. This is a lasting friendship based on old-fashioned loyalty.

### Cancer Woman/Libra Friends

These pals are amiable enough, but both are slow to make important decisions—or even simple ones. They'll have fun together—but they might not get much done!

### Cancer Woman/Scorpio Friends

The Crab and the Scorpion are often drawn into a deep, intense friendship. Knowing that their tough shells protect very soft interiors, they are cautious but permanent pals.

## Cancer Woman/Sagittarius Friends

As long as no strings are attached, this friendship will flourish. But if Cancer cannot fulfill her need for security and control elsewhere, Sagittarius will quickly exit.

## Cancer Woman/Capricorn Friends

Cancer is typically somewhat temperamental; Capricorn is impatient with emotional displays. They operate in different realms—and are often uncomfortable together.

### Cancer Woman/Aquarius Friends

Intuitive Cancer and cerebral Aquarius often find themselves somewhat at odds. The Crab's snappishness and the Water Bearer's detachment may increase this distance.

### Cancer Woman/Pisces Friends

Both are happily at home in the mysterious undercurrents of emotions and intuition. This pair of watery pals amuses, supports, and truly understands each other.

# The Cancer Woman in Love

Affectionate, seductive, and romantic, the typical Cancerian woman blossoms when her passionate relationship is on the fast track to long-term commitment. But no matter how smitten she is, she may put her potentially significant other through a battery of romantic loyalty tests. Why? Because the dreamy (and vulnerable) Moon Maiden has learned to protect her precious emotions. She leaps carefully into love, but once she invites a man into her life, the bliss can last a lifetime.

Her charming unpredictability will keep her partner on his toes, and her tenderness will soothe him. So what if she tends to be clinging, demanding, and possessive? The right mate will understand that this behavior springs from insecurity—and will provide both the love in the heart *and* money in the bank to keep her purring contentedly forever.

# Cancer Woman/
# Aries Man

Can a watery, emotionally charged Cancerian woman find lasting happiness with an Aries man? Will she subtly cool his fiery passion to a slow, steady burn and then luxuriate in steamy romance, or will she drown him in her moody sensitivity?

Remember, Aries is the infant of the zodiac and requires constant love and attention. He thrives on challenges and he absolutely needs to explore. His work in life, he often feels, is to build a bright, shining ego and then take it into as many dramatic, action-packed scenarios as time permits. And the Aries motto is "I will."

Now consider the Cancerian woman. She typically needs to be pampered and reassured of her partner's love. She prizes fidelity, security, and an old-fashioned intimacy that usually begins with the words "I do." Sensitive and intuitive, she cannot help but absorb the psychic environment around her.

Just when she most needs her Aries

man, he's likely to be admiring himself in the nearest mirror. And just when he decides a night on the town (solo) is just what the doctor ordered for his restlessness, she suffers an attack of insecurity. She clings. He mutters a thoughtless Aries comment in her direction. She bursts into tears. He tries to make a joke (for he's often very witty). She cries harder.

But that's the worst of all possible scenarios! In fact, many Cancer/Aries couples have managed to ride the waves of love and lived to tell the tale. All it requires is careful attention—to each other! This is not easy for either one: Aries tends to be self-centered, and Cancer often gets walled in by her feelings. But if she can loosen her grip a bit and he can learn to curb his sharp tongue, they may discover a hot and sultry romantic world together—and live in it happily ever after.

# Cancer Woman/ Taurus Man

Deep in her heart, the typical Cancerian woman has a secret. She fervently longs for a strong man who can provide her with emotional (and financial) security— and a sensual, satisfying sex life too. In her dreams, this perfect mate would delight in the domestic life, be excessively cautious but courageous, and enjoy her tendency toward emotional dependence and occasional flare-ups of romantic jealousy.

Along comes the typical Taurus male. To her delight and amazement, he seems to fit the bill perfectly. Placid, easy-going, and patient, the Taurean man finds Cancer's Moon-inspired moods (which might intimidate others) mysteriously charming. He responds warmly to her kind, sympathetic nature. They notice that they share a love of creature comforts, cash in the bank, and long-term commitments.

But that's not all. The Taurus man is ruled by Venus, the goddess of love. This gives him a sexy, romantic edge, which is often irresistible to the dreamy Cancerian Moon Maiden. With his direct, determined approach to love and his long-term persistence, he is able to topple her emotional defenses. This is probably because the Taurus male is rarely casual in love—and the Cancerian woman instinctively knows it. Permanence is his middle name.

As for the Cancerian woman, she deeply values the quiet strength of astrology's favorite Bull. She allows him to see her vulnerability because he typically can be trusted. In fact, she usually enjoys being lured out of her personal shell, knowing that she will be protected from harm forever after.

This is a romantic pairing with compatibility built in. The Cancer woman happily sprinkles her mystical waters over the relationship. It seeps into the Taurus man's psyche, fertilizing an abundant, deep-rooted love that has every chance of turning their romantic life into an earthly Garden of Paradise.

# Cancer Woman/
# Gemini Man

When a Cancerian woman and a Gemini man become romantically entangled, the challenges usually fall into the "depth versus velocity" category. Cancer thrives in an atmosphere of mystery and intimate connection. She is most at home in her own emotions. She tends to fall in love slowly and rarely reveals even the very least of her many secrets.

The Gemini man, on the other hand,

is the zodiac's speed demon. Not only is he ruled by Mercury, the planet of quick, concise communication, he's also an air sign … and a Twin. Given his astrological profile, it's the most natural thing in the world that he is driven to analyze, categorize, and explain. But despite his facility with words and his lively mind, he cannot find a mental compartment for the dreamy Cancer woman.

So what happens when the Crab feels the urge to pair up with the Twins? Usually, the two (or is it three?) partners experience a sense of intoxicating wonderment

. . . soon followed by frustration that may quickly grow out of all proportion.

Part of the trouble will no doubt arise from Gemini's typically fickle nature. This is quite opposite to the Cancerian woman's romantic aims, which usually include permanence. Yet if she tries to hold on, as the Crab is prone to do, Gemini will most likely perform a vanishing act, churning up Cancer's emotional waters and causing her to withdraw into her shell.

The Gemini man, typically uncomfortable in the realm of the feelings, is often unable to coax her out again. And he doesn't usually stick around when the romantic going gets tough. The security-minded Cancerian woman is too emotionally vulnerable to put up with the Twins' fleet-footed antics for very long.

The prognosis on this match is questionable. The good news is that love miracles happen all the time. The bad news: These two will probably need one!

# Cancer Woman/ Cancer Man

Imagine two crabs on a beautiful beach. They happen to glance in each other's direction and a spark of familiar delight ignites. But each one scuttles sideways, away from the potential partner. Why risk rejection? Why risk heartache? Then the tide rolls in, carrying them close to one another. They sit silently and assess their feelings. There's a natural understanding between them, and the Moon is shimmering above. Suddenly the "Why try?" is replaced by "Why not?" . . . and they live happily ever after.

This is perhaps a slight exaggeration, but even in jest, there's more than a little truth. When a male and a female Crab meet, they are often amazed at the deep and immediate connection. Perhaps it's their essential ease in adapting to sudden mood changes. Or the instant recognition of their mutual vulnerability.

This watery pair is often magnetically attracted—probably the work of the Moon, which rules them both. But this does not always mean smooth sailing. Since each partner craves pampering, attention, and frequent displays of affection, one or the other will occasionally feel neglected and undervalued. And because both tend to be hypersensitive, hurt feelings and emotional wounds are bound to occur. Add to that the fact that their emotional tides may not be in sync, and the result is a life of ups and downs that might, at times, become exhausting.

But like the sea, the daily fluctuations rarely change the annual average, and Crabs are used to both the calm and the occasional storm. If each partner can manage to be a little more independent and a little less demanding, the chance for a meaningful, permanent, and essentially happy union is very likely.

Cancer/Cancer couples be warned: You are most at home in the depths of your shared psyches. But don't lose yourselves in deep reflection. Come up every now and then and look around!

# Cancer Woman/
## Leo Man

The typical Cancerian woman, ruled by
the Moon, is moody and reflective. Leo,
ruled by the Sun, likes to beam from cen-
ter stage at all times, and is happiest when
he's certain that his magnetic cheer is
warming everyone in the room. But can he
reach the cool, cautious Moon Maiden?

Absolutely. This is a unique water/fire
combination that has the potential to
get quite steamy. The secret lies with the

Cancerian woman's ability to reflect Leo back at twice his normal size. His notorious vanity cannot help but be flattered, and he may spend some quality private time admiring his larger-than-life image.

And the best part of all is that the Cancerian is being perfectly truthful in her admiration. Once she learns that his exuberant, openhearted personality is real, she tends to be powerfully drawn into his kingdom of optimism—a welcome change of scene for the moody Moon Maiden.

But it's probably Leo's strength that initially attracts her. With her tendency toward both insecurity and emotional fluctuations, the Cancer woman often perceives the Lion as a beacon of fiery power. And he is.

Of course, there may be times when his overbearing personality and, even worse, his dogmatic opinions (Leo is a fixed sign, after all) will intimidate the gentle, shy Cancerian woman. But when she gets tearful, Leo's heart will melt and he will typically find a way to apologize—and not necessarily with words.

Cancer's nit-picking worries about money will sometimes dampen Leo's fire a bit. So will her vagueness and her attachment to each and every part of her past. Leo may blow up, but his anger also blows over. And once Cancer's crying is done, they can quickly get back on track.

Both Cancer and Leo stand to get exactly what they need in this interesting Sun/Moon pairing. Leo can shine forth, and Cancer can move gracefully through her moods—a perfect mix of solar excitement and lunar stability.

# Cancer Woman/
# Virgo Man

The Cancerian woman, eternally able to renew herself and those around her, takes a stroll in the silvery light of her ruling planet, the Moon. She happens upon a Virgo man. As astrology's Virgin, this man is suspicious of romantic flutterings and prone to prefer permanent bachelorhood over the rigors of daily life with a partner.

But there is definitely an attraction. Earthbound as he is, he appreciates the nourishing drops of Cancer's watery emotions. He soaks them up and typically feels a lightening of his own deeply buried feelings. He's usually afraid of emotion because it threatens the control he feels compelled to display (and that he secretly dreads may not be real). But somehow he feels safe with her.

The Cancerian woman typically understands his caution in the romantic arena. She, too, is cautious, but for different reasons. She's more likely to fear that she won't be able to express her heartfelt emotions; he's afraid of showing his.

Somehow, the Moon Maiden and the Virgin recognize that they are on the same wavelength. Both might lower their defenses, inch by inch.

If the Virgin will stand still long enough, and the Cancerian woman can make her way (indirectly and Crab-like, of course) near enough, the chances of finding common ground and buried water are excellent. Both are affectionate, security minded, and private. Where Cancer tends to be dependent, Virgo is likely to be protective. Virgo is extremely analytical, but Cancer's powers of perception will often bring her to the same conclusion—and she doesn't have to be first.

Even romantic trouble spots are similar between this Moon/Mercury pairing. Both tend to chip away at partners during weak moments. But if Cancer can control her nagging and Virgo keeps his criticism to himself, these two can develop a mutual admiration that endures, despite surface differences, for a lifetime.

# Cancer Woman/ Libra Man

Put a Cancer woman and a Libra man together. Add up the good parts. They are both creative, imaginative, and witty. They need tenderness, sentimentality, and kindness. Both are given to daydreaming. They view it as a pleasant form of longing, and they often wish their dreams right into reality.

If it sounds as if the road to romance is paved with possibility for the Cancer/

Libra match, it is … and it isn't. True love, however, can transcend difficulties, which is good news for this particular pairing. Forewarned is forearmed!

The first problem: This is a water/air combination. In spirit, the Cancerian woman is heavy and the Libra man is light. He worships logic. Born under the sign of the Scales, he absolutely must intellectually weigh and measure each idea, action, or behavior. (Notice the word *feeling* is missing from the list.)

The watery Cancerian woman typically relies solely on her intuition and her sharp powers of perception, which cannot be explained to the Libra man. And she tends to perceive him as detached and emotionally unavailable. He usually is. So, she wonders, how can he help her investigate her mysterious depths? How can he be comfortable in her uncharted waters? He usually can't.

Cancer the Crab dreams of a cozy home, with her mate happily in it. Libra tends to feel trapped—even if he's not. He needs fresh air and new experience to fortify himself. When he disappears, his Cancer mate will probably take a nosedive into her basic insecurity. But if she complains, he may become logical and try to explain away her feelings—the very last thing the typical Cancerian woman wants.

But these are merely small personality hurdles to fly over—or swim under. If the passion grows despite the pitfalls, it's time to accept the inevitable. It may not be easy, but when a Cancer/Libra match works, it's truly transcendent.

# Cancer Woman/ Scorpio Man

What might encourage a self-protective Crab woman to suddenly reveal her sweet, vulnerable interior? Or motivate a Scorpio man to permanently put away his stinger and simply trust that he is safe with a potential mate?

Each other, of course.

This is a romantic match made in astrology's deepest waters. And when Cancer's sensuality meets Scorpio's unapologetic passion, the result is often a lovefest of unparalleled proportions.

Perhaps it's because they have so very much in common. Both have developed a tough exterior to protect a fragile but passionate interior. Both are highly intuitive, feeling oriented, and security minded. But the best match in astrology occurs when the weaknesses of each sign somehow complement each other and transform themselves into strengths. (Remember, Scorpio is ruled by Pluto, the planet of transformation.)

How does this display itself in a Cancer/

Scorpio pairing? It's simple. She is typically insecure and possessive. This often irritates potential partners, but not Scorpio. Why? Because he tends to be tortured by jealousy and fears of disloyalty and betrayal. Cancer's reliance on him is a near-constant reminder of her love. This soothes him. Over time, he abandons his fears and relaxes, a most unusual (and pleasant) experience for a Scorpio man.

Meanwhile, the Cancerian woman is frequently accused of carrying changeability to the point of hysteria. But strong, watery Scorpio understands her Moon cycles, and remains pleasantly amused (or at least unfazed) by her rapid mood changes and occasional snappishness. She relaxes. It feels like the acceptance she has dreamed of—and it is.

And the grand finale: Both are home oriented, faithful, and built to sail safely through even the stormiest romantic waters. Is there anything more to ask for?

# Cancer Woman/ Sagittarius Man

Sagittarius, the Archer, inserts an arrow into his bow, takes careful aim, and lets it fly. The Cancerian woman sees it coming, and, like the Crab she is, takes evasive action, charging first in one direction and then the next—even if she's completely intrigued.

In fact, she may be quite enamored of the Sagittarius man. Ruled by Jupiter, the planet of expansion, success, and generosity, he comes on like gangbusters.

She responds to his high-spirited fire with a silvery, Moon-like shiver. He's obviously an explorer, and the Cancerian woman can't help but imagine him taking the swan dive into love—with her. They could probably redefine the phrase "hot and sultry."

The Archer loves to talk, and the Cancerian woman is an excellent listener. But as he outlines (in detail) his dreams and goals, she is busy fantasizing a future home life together. This is where the communication becomes strained, for the Sagittarius man typically follows the "no strings attached" philosophy, and "foot-loose" is his most cherished self-image. He not only resents any sign of dependence in his mate, he is bored by it. Should he display these feelings, he is bound to receive either tears or crankiness from the typical Crab.

And then there's money. The Crab likes to get it and hold on to it. Sagittarius tends to be extravagant, believing eternally in his ability to produce more (of anything, not just cash) on demand. The Cancerian woman longs for the trappings of security—a nice home filled with mementos and memories. The Archer tends to scoff at tradition. He'd rather gamble than settle down.

But if the Crab can control her jealousy and the Archer can tone down (just a little!) his traveling ways, the potential for a water/fire mix that boils happily for years is good. All it takes is a little self-control, which would benefit both the Cancerian woman and her Sagittarius partner.

# Cancer Woman/ Capricorn Man

The Cancer woman and the Capricorn man begin with a favorable edge in the great game of love and romance: They're astrological opposites. And like all opposites, they are attracted to each other for good reasons. Each secretly suspects that the other can supply the key that will unlock both their hearts. For the watery Crab and the earthy Goat, this may very well be true.

For starters, both are oriented toward home, family, and financial security. Because the Goat tends to be conservative, he expects to fulfill the traditional masculine roles: protector, provider, and leader. The Cancerian woman is more than willing to follow—if she feels that her mate's love is genuine.

She typically views her Capricorn man as a pillar of strength, something solid to cling to as she moves through her personal lunar phases. Capricorn doesn't mind. A worker at heart (even in the field of romance), he considers it all part of his job.

Because both the Goat and the Crab are born collectors, there is no tension as the house fills with mementos from bygone days (or even eras). Capricorn's motto, "I use," says it all. The Cancerian woman can finally luxuriate in her attachments instead of apologizing for them.

Capricorn does, however, feel the occasional need to retreat into himself. But who can better understand this than the Crab? Though the Cancerian woman may sometimes feel blocked out, it usually means her mate is occupied in planning his next career move. When the Goat temporarily forgets to pamper his Moon Maiden, she should remind herself that his periodic withdrawals are usually followed by even more security.

A strong man and a devoted woman often find romantic happiness together. The Cancerian woman can supply the mystery and the Capricorn man the reality. And in secret, they exchange their gifts. Doubters please note: There is a logic to "opposites attract" after all.

# Cancer Woman/ Aquarius Man

Is Aquarius, the Water Bearer, truly an *air* sign? How can a man who adores the mystery of the Moon Maiden exhibit such antilunar inflexibility? Why does he resent the Crab's minor displays of possessiveness when it's crystal clear to both of them that they could happily soar to romantic heights and dive to emotional depths together?

These are the questions the typical

Cancerian woman might ask herself when she's about to tumble into love with an Aquarian man. She'll probably ask him too. He'll answer logically—or at least he will think so. But what passes for logic with Aquarius might be viewed as a positively eccentric thought pattern to the next person.

That doesn't deter the Cancerian woman. She finds Aquarius's oddball take on life to be charming, perhaps because his unpredictability is not so very different from her own. Of course, hers is feminine and Moon-inspired. His is masculine, attributable to his ruling planet, Uranus. Still, it feels familiar to the Cancerian woman—and familiarity is her constant comfort.

This couple will face the usual water/air problems. He is independent by nature, while she tends to cling. The Aquarius man is terribly fixed in his opinions, while the Cancerian woman is typically flexible (and prone to feeling bullied). He lives in his head while she usually acts directly from the heart.

But both Aquarius and Cancer love to disappear into private flights of fancy—

his, airborne, and hers, dreamy and waterlogged. And Cancer, usually so possessive, rarely feels threatened by her Aquarian's downtime. In fact, she often wishes he'd take a bit more of it, just so she could bask in her own moonbeams.

As they grow older, the Aquarius man and the Cancerian woman become more alike. He settles down a bit. She begins to explore. There's never a dull moment for this pair, from the first to the last.

# Cancer Woman/ Pisces Man

Peace, harmony, intimacy, true love—the typical Cancerian woman is likely to repeat this mantra to herself as she prays for her other half to find her. And he may be swimming toward her through a sea of emotions, feelings, and intuitions, right at this moment. Pisces, the Fish, can usually hear her call, even if she barely whispers it. Even if she only thinks it. Why? Because it is so very nearly his own.

The Crab and the Fish happily coexist in the watery romantic realm. They are well matched in passion potential and comfortable in the great mystery of love. They are sensitive, tuned-in, and appreciative of each other. In fact, they are so essentially similar that they often float along for extended periods with no whirlpools whatsoever to set them off course.

Until they come to the proverbial "black hole," that is. For this particular pair, the trouble spots are melancholy and depression. If one partner succumbs, however temporarily, to these watery traps, the other will tend to absorb it, mirror it, and carry it even further. This can spiral both of them deeper and deeper, until it may seem impossible to rise up and escape.

But if the Cancerian woman keeps her head, she can offer a helping hand to her Pisces mate. Just being affectionate and sensitive may cause his dark cloud to dissolve. And once it does, his imaginative charm is bound to bewitch her.

And if the Pisces man sees his Crab retreat into her shell, he must coax her out again. Words of love, a gift that says, "I'll always love you," even a promise to be a bit more careful with his cash will often do the trick.

The outlook is good for this lucky water couple. They may just get their wish—to experience total harmony, revel in romance, and learn the greatest mystery of them all: that passion, perfectly expressed, brings peace.

# Watery Cancer Woman

## DIANA FRANCES SPENCER (PRINCESS DIANA)

*July 1, 1961–August 31, 1997*

Perhaps the deepest secret of the typical Cancerian woman is her unquenchable thirst for love. She tends to feel that emotional security is the most important factor leading to happiness.

Princess Diana, adored by millions of people all around the world but unhappy in her own marriage, is one such Cancerian woman. From her fairy-tale courtship to her tragic death at the age of thirty-six, she longed, in public and in private, for the security that the Crab can only find in a happy home and family life.

Born to an aristocratic family, Diana's early life was one of privilege. But her sensitivity shone through, particularly in her Cancerian love of children. Before her grand marriage, she was a nanny and a kindergarten teacher.

When Prince Charles, the future king of England, proposed marriage, Diana was just nineteen years old. Bringing grace, vitality, and a truly Cancerian sense of caring, she captured hearts around the world and created a new image for the royal family. When she gave birth to two sons of her own, William and Harry, it seemed as if her Cancerian dreams had come true.

Unfortunately, however, her marriage crumbled. Diana maintained her dignity —and her honor—when she rejected her loveless marriage and accepted the terms of a very public divorce. A true Cancer, she called herself the "Queen of Hearts" and continued her work for many charitable organizations and causes.

Though several relationships failed, Diana apparently found true love with international businessman Dodi Fayed. It is truly a cruel twist of fate that their life together was cut short when they both perished in a tragic car accident.

At Diana's funeral, her brother commented, "Diana remained a very insecure person at heart"—truly a Cancerian trait. Through all the privilege and honors, beneath her generosity, kindness, and beauty, Diana longed for happiness and was intensely private and very human.